Community Helpers
and Their Tools

# A Landscaper's Tools

## Sebastian Avery

**PowerKiDS**
press.

New York

Published in 2016 by The Rosen Publishing Group, Inc.
29 East 21st Street, New York, NY 10010

First Edition

Editor: Caitie McAneney
Book Design: Reann Nye

Photo Credits: Cover (background) Ozgur Coskun/Shutterstock.com; cover (man) michaeljung/Shutterstock.com; p. 5 Christian Delbert/ Shutterstock.com; pp. 6, 21 (dust mask) Ispace/Shutterstock.com; pp. 6, 21 (gloves) Florin Burlan/Shutterstock.com; pp. 6, 21 (saftey glasses) PodPad/Shutterstock.com; p. 7 ChameleonsEye/Shutterstock.com; pp. 8, 21 (shovel) Andrey Eremin/ Shutterstock.com; p. 8 (wheelbarrow) James Marvin Phelps/Shutterstock.com; pp. 8, 21 (trowel) Praisaeng/Shutterstock.com; p. 9 Christina Richards/Shutterstock.com; pp. 10, 21 (pickax) pryzmat/Shutterstock.com; pp. 10, 21 (hoe) Andrew Burgess/ Shutterstock.com; p. 11 Erika J Mitchell/Shutterstock.com; pp. 12, 21 (weed whacker) Jaimie Duplass/Shutterstock.com; pp. 12, 21 (leaf blower) jocic/Shutterstock.com; p. 13 Vadim Ratnikov/Shutterstock.com; p. 14 Chris Roselli/Shutterstock.com; p. 15 B Brown/Shutterstock.com; pp. 16, 21 (watering can) Alexander Raths/Shutterstock.com; pp. 16, 21 (hose) eurobanks/ Shutterstock.com; p. 17 Candus Camera/Shutterstock.com; pp. 18, 21 (pruning saw) Serg64/Shutterstock.com; pp. 18, 21 (bow saw) Vadym Zaitsev/Shutterstock.com; p. 19 Wallenrock/Shutterstock.com; pp. 20, 21 (auger) vallefrias/ Shutterstock.com; p. 21 (bulldozer) Smileus/Shutterstock.com; p. 21 (backhoe) dragon_fang/Shutterstock.com; p.21 (headphones) Kellis/Shutterstock.com; p. 21 (vest) Volodymyr Krasyuk/Shutterstock.com; p. 21 (tractor) stefan11/Shutterstock.com; p. 21 (edger) travelpixpro/E+/Getty Images; p. 21 (lawn mower) risteski goce/Shutterstock.com; p. 21 (rotary tiller) Toa55/Shutterstock.com; p. 21 (sprinkler) keerati/Shutterstock.com; p. 21 (loppers) ajt/Shutterstock.com; p. 21 (spade) Sergio Schnitzler/Shutterstock.com; p. 22 © iStockphoto.com/ IPGGutenbergUKLtd.

Library of Congress Cataloging-in-Publication Data

Avery, Sebastian, author.
 A landscaper's tools / Sebastian Avery.
     pages cm. — (Community helpers and their tools)
Includes bibliographical references and index.
ISBN 978-1-4994-0853-9 (pbk.)
ISBN 978-1-4994-0857-7 (6 pack)
ISBN 978-1-4994-0899-7 (library binding)
1. Landscape architects—Juvenile literature. 2. Landscape gardening—Juvenile literature. I. Title. II. Series: Community helpers and their tools.
SB469.37.A94 2015
635.9—dc23
                              2015009898

Manufactured in the United States of America

CPSIA Compliance Information: Batch #WS15PK: For Further Information contact Rosen Publishing, New York, New York at 1-800-237-9932

# Contents

# The Great Outdoors

Have you ever stopped and enjoyed the trees and gardens in your local park? There may have been beautiful **shrubs**, trees, and plants. There may have even been walls, walkways, and decorations. These beautiful outdoor spaces were likely built and **maintained** by landscapers.

Landscapers work on outdoor spaces from backyards to national parks. They keep the grounds looking clean and colorful. They keep plants and grass growing and cut them when they get too big. Landscapers have the help of many important tools.

## TOOL TIME!

If you want to design, or plan, outdoor spaces, you can go to school to be a landscape **architect**. They design parks, gardens, zoos, and more.

Do you like spending time outside?
You might enjoy a job as a landscaper.

# What to Wear

Landscaping can be a dirty job! Many landscapers wear jeans or other pants they don't mind getting dirty. If they're working near roads or construction **sites**, they might wear a bright vest so drivers and workers can see them.

Gloves keep a landscaper's hands safe and clean and give them a better hold on tools. Some landscapers wear glasses or goggles to **protect** their eyes. Sometimes landscapers have to wear a dust mask over their nose and mouth to keep from breathing in dust and other matter.

## TOOL TIME!

Landscapers who use chainsaws sometimes wear protective aprons, pants, shirts, or gloves. They're made of special **material** that can't be cut by the saw.

gloves

safety glasses

dust mask

Power tools can be loud! Landscapers sometimes use special headphones to block the noise when they use power tools.

# Dig In!

Landscapers are careful to put plants in just the right places. When they find the right place, they have to dig a hole to fit the plant. They might use a shovel for this, which has a long handle and a large, slightly curved blade. They might use a spade, which usually has a smaller, flatter blade.

Landscapers also use trowels, which are hand tools with a pointed, curved blade and a handle. Trowels are used for digging small holes and turning the dirt over.

## TOOL TIME!

Landscapers use wheelbarrows to carry dirt, rocks, and other matter from place to place.

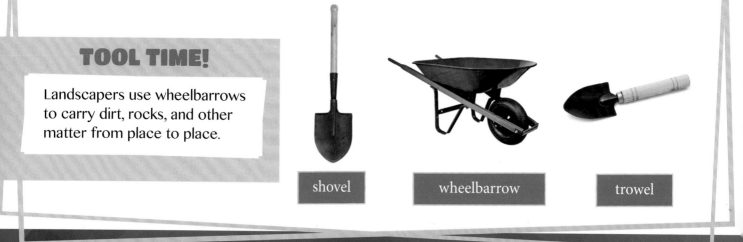

shovel     wheelbarrow     trowel

Landscapers have to dig larger holes for planting trees. They can use a spade or shovel. A trowel might be used to plant something smaller.

# Breaking Up Dirt

Sometimes landscapers need to break up a large area of soil to make it ready for planting. This keeps the soil healthy and removes weeds. Hoes are tools that have been used for thousands of years to break up soil. They have a long handle and a head with a flat blade on an angle. Landscapers hit the dirt with the blade and drag it.

If the ground is very hard and dry, a landscaper might need to use a pickax. A pickax has a head with a sharp point on either end.

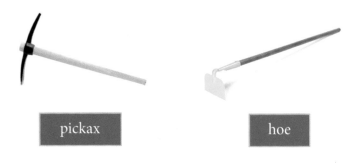

pickax

hoe

## TOOL TIME!

Breaking up soil is called cultivating. Cultivating soil makes it easier for plants to grow.

Breaking up soil is also called tilling. A rotary tiller, also known as a rototiller, has sharp teeth that spin and break up the soil. Many are powered by engines.

# Green and Clean

Landscapers work to make grass look green and clean. They need to plant seeds in some places to make grass grow. Some landscapers even roll new grass out like a carpet!

Sometimes grass grows quickly, and in that case, landscapers need to mow it. A lawn mower is a machine that uses turning blades to cut grass to an even height. Some lawn mowers are pushed by hand, while others are powered by engines. Some lawn mowers are built so you can drive them.

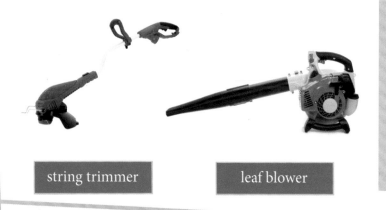

string trimmer

leaf blower

## TOOL TIME!

Landscapers sometimes use rakes to remove leaves from grass. They also use leaf blowers. These power tools blow air through a tube, which blows leaves out of the way.

Landscapers use power tools called string trimmers, or "weed whackers," to trim high grass and weeds. They use power tools called edgers to cut grass along the edge of a walkway.

# Spraying and Spreading

Some lawns stay green and healthy because landscapers spray fertilizers on them. Fertilizer is a **chemical** that helps plants grow. Some landscapers use liquid fertilizer to spray over lawns. Others use a broadcast spreader, which is a tool that spreads **granular** fertilizer when you push it.

Some bugs are harmful to plants. Landscapers sometimes use pesticides, which are also called insecticides. These are chemicals that keep certain bugs away. Landscapers apply the pesticides to flowerbeds, grass, and other areas they want to keep safe from bugs.

broadcast spreader

Landscapers may also spray or spread herbicides, or chemicals that kill weeds, such as dandelions.

# Plants Need Water!

Plants need water to grow and stay healthy. Landscapers need to water lawns and gardens to keep them growing. Landscapers can use a hose, which is a thin tube hooked up to a water system. Hoses bring water to where it's needed.

Some landscapers set up water systems called sprinkler systems in outdoor places. Landscapers **install** sprinklers in the ground. They're attached to either an outdoor water tap or a full **plumbing** system. Sprinklers water the ground evenly.

watering can

hose

## TOOL TIME!

A great tool for watering smaller gardens and plants is a watering can!

Some landscaping companies hire irrigation specialists to work on water systems. Irrigation specialists plan and install sprinkler systems.

# Just a Trim

Landscapers shape what an outdoor space looks like. To do that, they need to trim the trees, shrubs, and other plants in their workspace. This is also called pruning, which means cutting off unwanted parts of a plant.

There are a few important tools for trimming trees. Loppers are like long scissors. When you push the handles together, two blades come together to cut something. The long handles on loppers help landscapers reach high branches.

## TOOL TIME!

A pruning saw is a thin saw that's used to cut twigs and branches. A bow saw looks like a bow, but it has sharp teeth for cutting thick branches.

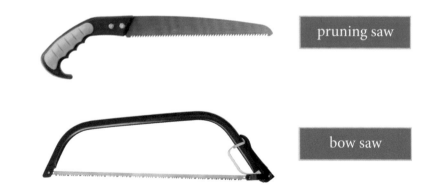

pruning saw

bow saw

This landscaper uses a tool called pruning shears to trim a tree.

# Start Your Engines!

Sometimes landscapers need to bring in the big tools to get the job done. Landscapers often use tractors to landscape large areas of land. Tractors are slow-moving **vehicles** that landscapers drive. Landscapers attach tools to the tractor to do a certain job. For example, landscapers can attach wide rakes to remove leaves and weeds.

Big tools called backhoes excavate, or remove dirt and stones. Backhoes have a long, folding arm connected to a bucket. Backhoes are sometimes attached to a tractor.

## TOOL TIME!

This tractor has an auger attached to it. An auger drills holes into the ground for planting trees and making fences.

# A Landscaper's Tools

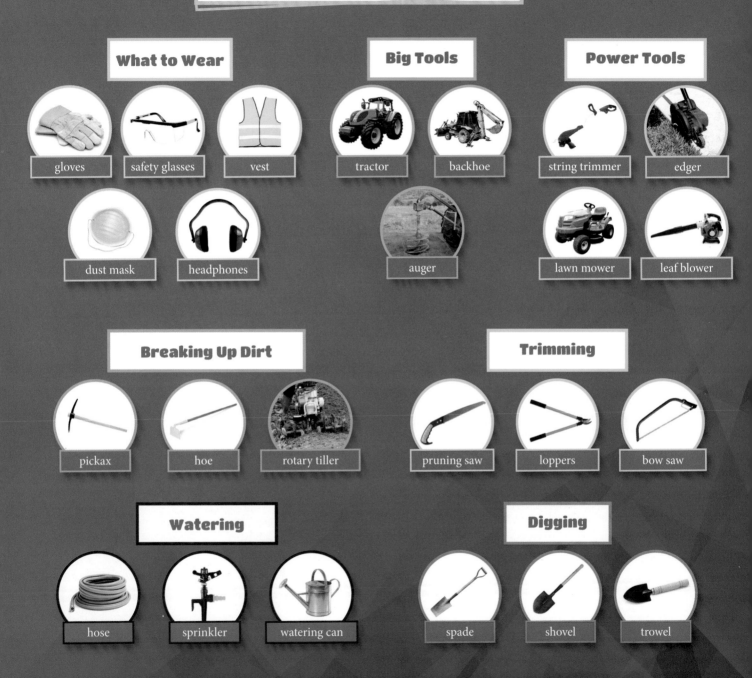

**What to Wear**
- gloves
- safety glasses
- vest
- dust mask
- headphones

**Big Tools**
- tractor
- backhoe
- auger

**Power Tools**
- string trimmer
- edger
- lawn mower
- leaf blower

**Breaking Up Dirt**
- pickax
- hoe
- rotary tiller

**Trimming**
- pruning saw
- loppers
- bow saw

**Watering**
- hose
- sprinkler
- watering can

**Digging**
- spade
- shovel
- trowel

21

# Landscaping Jobs

The next time you're at your local park, think about how landscapers have shaped the land. Landscapers are community helpers because they make community spaces beautiful. Do you think you'd like to work in landscaping? Jobs in landscaping include landscape architect, irrigation specialist, crew member, and **foreperson**.

Landscapers use their tools to make outdoor spaces that look healthy and colorful. Some landscapers build and maintain brick walkways and statues inside a garden. Some build and maintain ponds. Landscapers help us enjoy nature!

# Glossary

**architect:** A person who plans buildings or grounds.

**chemical:** Matter that can be mixed with other matter to cause changes.

**foreperson:** A person who is in charge of a group of workers.

**granular:** Made up of many small pieces, or grains.

**install:** To set something up to be used.

**maintain:** To care for something by making repairs and changes when needed.

**material:** Something made of matter. Also, something used to make something else.

**plumbing:** A system of pipes that carries water through a building.

**protect:** To keep safe.

**shrub:** A bush.

**site:** A place where a building stands or where something is being built.

**vehicle:** An object used for carrying people or goods.

# Index

**A**
auger, 20, 21

**B**
backhoes, 20, 21
bow saw, 18, 21
broadcast spreader, 14

**D**
dust mask, 6, 21

**E**
edgers, 13, 21

**F**
fertilizer, 14

**G**
glasses, 6, 21
gloves, 6, 21

**H**
headphones, 7, 21
herbicides, 15
hoes, 10, 21
hose, 16, 21

**I**
irrigation specialist, 17, 22

**L**
landscape architect, 4, 22
lawn mower, 12, 21
leaf blower, 12, 21
loppers, 18, 21

**P**
pesticides, 14
pickax, 10, 21
pruning, 18
pruning saw, 18, 21
pruning shears, 19

**S**
shovel, 8, 9, 21
spade, 8, 9, 21
sprinklers, 16, 17, 21
string trimmers, 13

**T**
tractors, 20, 21
trowel, 8, 9, 21

**V**
vest, 6, 21

# Websites

Due to the changing nature of Internet links, PowerKids Press has developed an online list of websites related to the subject of this book. This site is updated regularly. Please use this link to access the list: www.powerkidslinks.com/cht/land